Brian Hill

Henry and Acasto

A Moral Tale

Brian Hill

Henry and Acasto
A Moral Tale

ISBN/EAN: 9783744717465

Printed in Europe, USA, Canada, Australia, Japan

Cover: Foto ©Thomas Meinert / pixelio.de

More available books at **www.hansebooks.com**

HENRY and ACASTO:

A

MORAL TALE.

By the Rev. BRIAN HILL, A. M.

Late of Queen's College, Oxford;
And Chaplain to the Right Hon. the Earl of Leven.

With a PREFACE by Sir RICHARD HILL, Bart.

— — — — Quis talia fando
Temperet a lachrymis!—— VIRG.

LONDON:

Printed for JOHN STOCKDALE, oppofite Burlington
Houfe, Piccadilly;

Sold by J. MATHEWS, Strand; and T. WOOD,
Shrewfbury.

MDCCLXXXVI.

[Price One Shilling.]

[Entered at Stationers Hall.]

P R E F A C E.

IT may perhaps be thought, that par-
tiality towards a brother, or want of
judgment in myſelf, incline me to
think more highly of the following
poem than I ought to do, when I declare

clare that I don't remember ever to have met with any thing more pleaſing in the kind.   There is ſomething ſo intereſting in the ſtory itſelf, ſo delicate in the ſentiment, and ſo affectionate in the narration, that I am perſuaded it will not be read by many without awakening the moſt tender and refined ſenſations, and, I truſt, not without much improvement alſo.

To the religious mind it will be a farther recommendation to the poem, that it points out true chriſtianity as the only

thing

thing worth aiming at in life, and which can afford folid fupport in the hour of death; and if it tend in any meafure to correct the vitiated tafte of the day for compofitions of a dangerous and licentious nature, I fhall be the more fatisfied with the refolution I came to of making it public.

If there be fome ftrong expreffions in favor of virtue, they muft be underftood of that virtue only which is the fruit of faith, agreeable to the apoftle's exhortation, *add to your faith virtue* * :

virtue*: for it is fully evident by the ftriking manner in which the author paints the ftruggles between nature and grace in young Henry's mind, that whilft he (the author) acknowledges the intire depravity of all the children of Adam, he is convinced of the abfolute inefficacy of the united powers of reafon, fcience, and even of the moft refined leffons on the beauty of virtue and the deformity of vice, to change and convert the heart, independent of the influences of the divine Spirit.

* 2 Pet. i. 5.

I now

I now beg leave to add, that the author of the poem was totally ignorant of it's being sent abroad into the world. It was by mere accident that I first got a transient sight of it, and not till after repeated requests that I obtained a copy of it; and had I then intimated the most distant wish of printing it, (particularly with his name annexed,) I know that his great humility and diffidence would never have permitted him to let me have it in my possession: but as I feel conscious, that, whilst I render a service to the public, I do him no discredit, I venture to send it out in it's native simplicity.

By

By what I have lately heard the author drop on the subject, I have reason to believe that he meditates a second part, or rather another canto, which will bring the poem down to the death of ACASTO, and contain the remaining part of the history of HENRY; but when that will be finished, or whether it will ever be compleated at all, I take not upon me to determine. As to the lines which follow, they were chiefly compofed in fome folitary ftrolls which the author frequently took among fome pleafingly wild fcenes, not unlike thofe with a defcription of which the poem begins; but it was not till within

thefe

thefe few weeks that I faw a fingle word
of the performance.-

I had fome intentions of prefixing an
introductory argument to the work ; but
as the verfification is not of that fort as
to want continual explanatory notes, in
order to come at the author's meaning,
(a circumftance not very unfrequent in
poetry,) and as a profaic argument would
only tend to anticipate what is to follow,
and to prevent it's ftriking the mind with
that degree of force which it might do
when the ftory is fuffered to unfold itfelf

A 4   in

in the narration, I thought it better not
to foreſtal the reader's judgment by any
thing of the kind.

RICHARD HILL..

HARLEY-STREET,
June 1, 1786.

HENRY

HENRY AND ACASTO:

A MORAL TALE.

Where nature's scenes in wild confusion lie,

And cloud-capt mountains strike th' astonish'd eye;

Where bulging rocks their lofty summits show,

Whilst roaring torrents from their caverns flow,

And swift descending in unceasing foam

Glide thro' the dale to reach their briny home;

Where

Where forefts vaft their varied fhade combine,

Here th' aged oak, and there the fpiral pine;

Where the dark yew impends the chafm deep,

And gentler birches o'er the fountains weep,

Whilft many a moffy fragment, fteep'd in dew,

Meets the bright ray, and gliftens to the view:

Midft fcenes fo grand a lonely vale is found

Where fofter beauties deck the turfy ground;

Where banks reclining fhow their flow'ry fide,

And peaceful cattle from the tempeft hide.

Here good Acafto from the world had fled,

Wean'd from it's pleafures, to it's follies dead;

From error's paths he cautioufly withdrew,

And ftill more godlike as in years he grew;

Whilft

Whilft all his actions heav'nly wifdom fhow'd,

Unnumber'd graces in his bofom' glow'd;

There love divine, the firft of all the train,

And placid peace, their fix'd abode maintain;

There meeknefs, patience, gentlenefs and joy,

And faith and hope, and deep humility.

No longer now among the youths he fhone,

No longer now the prize of glory won;

Nor rais'd as erft by mighty deeds his fame,

When manly vigor ftrung his nervous frame.

Full oft had Phœbus run his yearly way,

Since firft Acaflo hail'd the light of day.

The mark of time his furrow'd vifage fhow'd,

And fnowy locks adown his fhoulders flow'd.

But

But tho' grave wifdom's characters he bore,

No rigid fternnefs on his afpect wore.

Not for himfelf this lone retreat he chofe,

Of cares diveft his remnant hours to lofe,

To fink in leifure's foft lethargic arms,

And fall a victim to her foothing charms.

Far nobler motives fway'd his gen'rous breaft;

And ftill to act the bufy part he prefs'd.

From the vain world he led a gentle youth,

Here to direct him in the paths of truth *;

Inftructive leffons to his foul impart,

Ere fubtle vice had won his eafy heart.

Faft by a rock that from the mountain ftood,

Whofe tufty fides were fring'd with brufhy wood,

Which

* Inter fylvas Academi quærere verum.

Which half conceal'd the dewy drop that fell

With filent trickle to the cryftal well,

A ruftic cottage, rais'd by artift mean,

In fweet fimplicity of .ftyle was feen.

No grand pilafters rofe in ftately pride,

No labor'd cornice grac'd it's humble fide ;

No fculptor's hand had wrought th' upolifh'd ftone,

Within it's walls no gilded cielings fhone.

Clofe at the threfhold fragrant woodbines grew,

And o'er it's fides luxuriant branches threw,

Whilft twifted ivy to the door-pofts clung,

And from the roof in gloffy curtains hung.

Small was the line that o'er th' uneven ground,

In form unheeded, mark'd it's utmoft bound.

'Twas

'Twas here Acaſto and his lovely boy

Securely liv'd in innocence and joy.

Nine times had ſpring the face of nature chear'd,

As oft had ſummer's gaudy train appear'd,

Nine times Autumna ſpread her golden ſtore,

And icy fields ſtern winter's garment wore,

Since pious Anna felt a mother's throes,

And the firſt light on Henry's head aroſe;

'When heav'n, all wiſe, th' afflictive mandate ſpoke,

And friends ſurviving felt the fatal ſtroke;

That ſtroke which Henry of his ſire bereſt,

And the ſweet child an helpleſs orphan left.

Then did Acaſto mark him for his own,

Wept o'er the ſmiling babe, and cried " My ſon !"

An

A MORAL TALE.

An happy lot the tender infant found,

Midſt friends for worth and piety renown'd ;

Friends that might watch his early ſteps, and ſhow

Th' unbeaten path in which a child ſhould go *.

Betimes his liſping tongue was taught to frame

With rev'rend awe his great Creator's name ;

His knees before th' eternal throne to bend,

And ſeek the bleſſings that a God could ſend.

Well did Acaſto all his tempers ſpy,

Trace ev'ry virtue, and each vice deſcry ;

Deep was he ſkill'd in learning's ſacred page,

His words were weighty, and his counſels ſage.

Young Henry liſten'd with attentive ear,

And, won by love or aw'd by filial fear,

* Prov. xxii, 6.

Felt all his leffons in his inmoft foul,

His paffions foften and his will controul.

Ne'er was the youth to ftudy's drudge confin'd,

No tedious precepts pall'd his tender mind;

But charm'd th' inftruftor's pleafing tale he caught,

And while he learnt the more to learn he fought.

Soon as Aurora's fmiling face was feen

And filver-fpangles deck'd the daify'd green;

Soon as the larks their early fong begun,

And thoufand cobwebs floated in the fun;

The twain would leave their humble roof and ftray

O'er Shepherds tracks their carelefs winding way,

To quaff frefh breezes of the pureft air,

And the rich bounties of creation fhare;

Whilft

Whilſt many a moral wiſe Acaſto drew

From each ſurrounding objeĉt in their view.

(As the foul ſoul with dunghill vapors gleams,

And poiſon ſips e'en from cœleſtial ſtreams,

The virtuous mind improves from all it meets,

And wiſdom's honey-culls from nature's ſweets.)

Thus would he mark ſome aged tree that ſtood

The priſtine monarch of the mighty wood,

It's rugged arms with foliage thinly ſpread,

And bow'd by wintry ſtorms it's batter'd head :

See there, my child, the ſage inſtruĉtor cried,

How ſhort a ſpace the firmeſt things abide !

That ſtem, by time's relentleſs hand defac'd,

For many a year it's native ſoil has grac'd :

B Unnum-

Unnumber'd children round the father rofe,

And barren foil extended woodland grows;

They flourish now, but foon themfelves fhall know

That vig'rous ftrength muft yield to age's blow.

'Tis thus with man——now health his frame fuftains,

Whilft youthful ardor in his bofom reigns;

But time attends, foon bows his hoary head,

And lays him proftrate with the conquer'd dead:

A race fucceeds, no longer fpace is given,

They fall obedient to the will of heaven.

Then prize not that which foon fhall be decay'd,

Nor court the grandeur which muft quickly fade.

Or fee yon' flow'r, which feels the genial ray,

And opes it's bofom to the beam of day,

Lends

Lends of it's fragrance to the paffing gale,

That gently wafts it thro' the balmy vale,

Shrinks at the evening blaft, and, ere the night

Flies from the arrows of returning light,

In fhrivel'd form now kifs the humid ground,

And fcarce it's traces in the morn are found.

Such may my Henry be; he lives to-day

Young, active, healthy, vigorous, and gay;

But ere the car of yon' declining fun

Shall from the gilded eaft once more have run,

His beating pulfe may ceafe, life's vapor fly,

And pallid Henry like that flow'ret lie.

Say then, my child, fhould foon the fummons come,

To call thy foul to it's eternal home,

Couldft

Couldſt thou undaunted ſtand the ſhock, nor dread

The gloomy manſions of the grave to tread ?

Would no ſad preſage of a judgment hour

In awful terrors o'er thy conſcience low'r ?

Well doſt thou know with what paternal care

For that dread day I charg'd thee to prepare ;

Show'd thee the chart that leads to Sion's land,

Preciſely mark'd by God's unerring hand.

That way purſue by inſpiration's ſide,

Nor let vain fancy's meteor be thy guide :

By fancy led, advent'rous Adam fell,

And bow'd ſubjection to the prince of hell.

His race corrupted in his footſteps trod ;

They fancied wiſdom, and they ſtray'd from God.

"_I am_

" *I am the way*," th' almighty Savior cries *;

By thee I go, the faithful foul replies.

'Tis thine my guilty foul from fin to fave,

And make thy ranfom'd triumph o'er the grave,

By thee I mount the glorious realms above,

To chaunt the praifes of redeeming love.

Tell me, my much-lov'd boy, are fuch thy views,

Or what the prize thy lab'ring foul purfues?

Prevent Acafto's fears that Henry's mind

To earth's vain joys alone fhould be confin'd.

Thus truth in many a pleafing garb array'd

The good inftruĉtor to his child convey'd:

Henry attentive heard, and whilft he fpoke,

Conviĉtion warm thro' all his foul awoke;

B 3   Reafon

* John xiv. 6.

Reafon enthron'd did all her right maintain,

And ftubborn felf confefs'd her high domain.

Now counfels paft their former weight acquir'd,

And ftrong refolves his yielding bofom fir'd.

But thefe, alas! juft as the meteor's gleam

Pours forth its bright but momentary ftream,

Strike on th' affections and commotion raife;

But foon extinguifh'd is the *crackling blaze*,

Quench'd by the ftreams which flow from pleafure's fpring,.

And frothy trifles in their courfes bring.

　　Acafto patient, ftill to teach intent,

O'er happier times with pleafing forefight bent,

Saw heav'n-born virtue, deck'd with native charms,.

Receive his Henry with extended arms;

　　　　　　　　　　　　　　　　Saw

Saw vice unmaſk'd, her hideous aſpect ſhown,

Her dev'liſh wiles, her dire enchantments known,.

Deſpis'd, abhorr'd, with all her helliſh train

Dragg'd to the manſions of eternal pain.

Still crafty vice in lurking ambuſh lay

To ſeize in fatal hour th' unwary prey;

Whilſt virtue watchful ſtood, and gently ſtrove

By ſoft perſuaſives to engage his love.

Vain the contention—the degen'rate mind,

By ſad propenſity to vice inclin'd,

Full oft the brittle cords of ſcience broke,

And ſnapp'd the feebler twigs of reaſon's yoke:

The ſeeds of inbred ſin, awhile conceal'd,

Warm'd by temptation's ſun, began to yield

Their copious fruits, whence baneful odors ſhed,

Fatal contagion all around them ſpread.

But good Acaſto, who at wiſdom's gate

Would oft in frame devout a ſuppliant wait *,

And taſte communion ſweet, whilſt love divine

Did o'er his ſoul with rays refulgent ſhine,

Implor'd th' Almighty by his pow'r to break

The barren ſoil of Henry's heart; then ſpeak

Fertility, and make *the fallow'd ground* †,

By ſhow'rs of grace, in heav'nly fruits abound.

 Once as the twain their wonted rambles took

In careleſs rovings by the pebbly brook,

The ſweets collecting that of faireſt hue

In rich profuſion on it's margin grew.

With

* Prov. viii. 34. † Jer. iv. 3. Hoſ. x. 12.

With nice diftinction of botanic art

Minutely viewing each component part,

The fleecy tribe, by blithfome fhepherds led,

Around them fearlefs on the verdure fed :

The fportive lambkin, from it's mother ftray'd,

It's fellows found, and thoufand gambols play'd :

The bleating dam, with tend'reft care opprefs'd,

Recall'd her darling to the milky breaft ;

Her darling heard and frifk'd with bounding pace

To tafte on bended knee the warm folace.

The pleafing fcene the youth's attention drew,

And ftrong amazement on his features grew :

Unmov'd he ftood, in deep reflection loft,

With anxious thought his lab'ring bofom toft.

The

The flow'rs no more his grafping hand adorn,

But drop neglected on the graffy lawn :

Some fighs efcap'd ; at length he filence broke,

And thus inquiring to Acafto fpoke :

　　Whence does it come, my kind protector, own,

Maternal care was ne'er to Henry known ?

Each lambkin vies with fond delight to prove

The foft endearments of a mother's love :

Thoughtlefs they feed beneath her watchful eye,

Nor fear they danger e'en when danger's nigh.

So the fweet thrufh, that fits on yonder fpray,

And charms my ears with her melodious lay,

Oft have I feen her downy neftlings brood,

And wing her way to feek their diftant food ;

　　　　　　　　　　　　　　　　　　But

But quick returning with far nobler ſtore

Than richeſt ſhip which ſails from India's ſhore,

An inſect p'rhaps or worm, the trophy ſpoil

Of all her warlike feats and buſy toil,

With beaks all ope her half fledg'd young ones ſoon

Receive with chirps of joy the captive boon.

   So too the boys, that from the village come,

And oft in parties thro' our valley roam,

Will ſpeak with tranſport of a mother's care,

And haſten back her tend'reſt love to ſhare.

Ah! 'why am I of ſuch delights bereft?

To ſooth my childhood why no mother left?

Could I in infancy neglected live,

Or would not heav'n the needful bleſſing give?

Say,

Say, gen'rous fire, for thou wilt not difdain

Such myft'ries great to Henry's mind t' explain.

   Mov'd was Acafto's foul, in deepeft thought

Aghaft he ftood; for painful mem'ry brought

Paft forrows back, and forc'd the tear to ftart

That fpoke the feelings of a wounded heart;

Yet foon his force refum'd, he filence broke

And thus to eager-looking Henry fpoke :

   Know, my dear child, fince thou canft wifely glean

Inftruction fweet from yon' expreffive fcene,

Know heav'n's myfterious ways, and patient wait -

Whilft I from times remote my tale relate.

   Bleft was the feafon of my youthful years,

By cares unclouded, unappall'd by fears :

                                          My.

My quiet breaft no piercing forrows tore,

No keen afflicion fway defpotic bore.

All was ferene. Thefe hands by bufy toil

The fruits collected of my fertile foil;

And tho' no bags o'erflow'd with golden ore,

Yet was. my table grac'd with plenteous ftore.

Kind heav'n was pleas'd a partner fair to fend,

A dear companion and a faithful friend;

In her all virtues met, and tho' in vain

. We feek perfection in this world to gain,

‹ In her no fpot appear'd, but richly giv'n

. Was ev'ry grace, and " *in her eye was heav'n.*"

~ One lovely babe engag'd our anxious care,

. Whofe weal we daily fought in focial pray'r:

Beneath

Beneath a mother's watchful eye she grew,

And shining virtues from her precepts drew.

As time roll'd on we saw fair Anna rise

In matchless worth to crown our earthly joys.

Such was our lot, 'mid sweets domestic fix'd,

Nor seem'd with human woes our portion mix'd.

No change I sought; when, ah! my chast'ning God

To me directed his afflicting rod.

My dear Selina—(scarce that name I speak,

But tears afresh bedew my aged cheek)—

My dear Selina droop'd beneath the pow'r

Of pale disease; to her in welcom'd hour

Death aim'd his blow, and gave the kind release

From sin and pain, and brought eternal peace.

Ne'er

Ne'er shall my soul forget her look serene,

My noblest solace in that awful scene :

Then with a smile she bid the world adieu,

Clos'd her fix'd eyes, and to her Savior flew.

Her fate I mourn not, but I mourn her loss;

The first my comfort, and the last my cross.

Much did my Anna feel, and vainly tried

With study'd care her struggling grief to hide;

Loud spoke the heaving sob, the stifled sigh;

The tear, that trembled in her cryftal'd eye,

Trac'd it's lone source from quick fensation's bed,

And wid'ning rose by springs of sorrow fed,

Burst it's fair banks by one o'erflowing swell,

Swept her sweet cheek, and on her bosom fell,

Till,

Till, drown'd in floods, around my neck fhe flung

Her fnowy arms, and on Acafto hung.

I can no more----Time's hand at length affuag'd

The troub'lous ftorm that in our bofoms rag'd.

Compofure mild, from heav'n infpir'd, arofe

In fweet fucceffion to our keener woes.

Anna her blooming prime had fcarce attain'd,

When thus on me the weighty charge remain'd.

Mov'd by the love which tender parents feel,

A thoufand fears my tranquil hours would fteal;

Fears left my child in fin's dark maze fhould ftray,

Tread pleafure's path, and mifs *the narrow way* *.

Ere long I faw a num'rous crowd attend;

At Anna's feet fubmiffive fuitors bend.

The

* Mat. vii. 13, 14.

The titled peer, for fplendor only fam'd,

In vain the ardor of his love proclaim'd :

The fop, of nought but empty found poffeft,

Declar'd with fruitlefs prate his aching breaft ;

Of beauteous Venus talk'd, of Cupid's darts,

Of fleeplefs, love-fick nights, and wounded hearts.

At length th' admiring throng Horatio join'd,

Of perfon pleafing, and of parts refin'd.

From early youth inur'd to war's campaigns,

He boldly ventur'd on the martial plains ;

Charg'd the dread foe, and wide the conqueft fpread,

As troops difmay'd his dauntlefs valor fled :

Humanely brave, whilft numbers round him fell,

His tender bofom would with pity fwell ;

C   The

The trembling captive own'd his gen'rous care

To eafe his burdens, and his forrows fhare.

Such was the youth who durft his love declare,

And prov'd fuccefsful with the yielding fair.

Their kindred fouls in fweeteft concord ftrung,

On ev'ry theme harmonic numbers rung:

The moiften'd eye would grief congenial fhow,

As oft they liften'd to the tale of woe:

From either's hand the lib'ral bounty fpread,

Chac'd deep diftrefs, and famifh'd orphans fed:

All virtue's paths with wary fteps they trod,

Gave men the profit, and the praife to God.

Whene'er remembrance of Selina's love

The finer paffions of my foul would move,

Horatio,

Horatio, kind, the heavy hours would chear,

And ſtop by converſe ſweet the falling tear.

Ere long I hail'd him ſon :—Indulgent heav'n

Sure greater bliſs had ne'er to parent giv'n

Than when I ſaw the brave Horatio's hand

With Anna's join'd in ſacred wedlock's band.

As rapid Time his ceaſeleſs journey went,

In ſweets domeſtic were our moments ſpent ;

Care with his comrades from our dwelling fled,

And thence his train to ſcenes of diſcord led ;

Whilſt peace, tranquillity, and love,

To raiſe our joys in kind contention ſtrove.

Still heav'n freſh bounties gave ; th' exulting pair

Expected ſoon the parent's charge to ſhare ;

C 2

With

With eager arms their love's sweet pledge embrace,

And each their likeness in the infant trace.

Thus were we blest, when noify rumour, fraught

With packets huge, the tale of horror brought,

Of leagues and schemes in foreign counfels plann'd,

Of pow'rful fleets by sturdy sailors mann'd ;

Of troops embark'd the glitt'ring sword to wield,

And try their valor in the glorious field :

Drums beat to arms ; our youth, inflam'd with zeal,

Flock'd to the standard for their country's weal.

Soon on our coasts, by vet'ran heroes led,

In ranks arrang'd, a num'rous army spread,

With force oppos'd to meet the hardy foe,

And feats of prowefs in the battle show.

There honor call'd my fon : fuch fad adieu

Ne'er love before fuftain'd, or forrow knew.

   In hideous forms now fleeplefs fancy walk'd,

And ghaftly phantoms o'er the moon-beams ftalk'd;.

Dear Anna's fwollen eye and pallid cheek

The inward language of her foul would fpeak;

Her waking thoughts on bloody flaughter run,

Her ftarting dreams proclaim'd the fight begun.

Struck by the blow of fome barbarian hand,

She paints Horatio breathlefs on the ftrand ;

Believes his bleeding corpfe amidft the boft

With trampled bodies in confufion loft.

Her fears too juft ; for tho' Horatio long

Scar'd with victorious arm th' embattled throng,.

       C 3,   . Thro'

Thro' thickeſt ranks by wiſe manœuvres broke,

Nor crav'd a reſpite from the frequent ſtroke,

Too far by valor urg'd, on ev'ry ſide

The preſſing foe at laſt his might defy'd.

Retreat was vain; deform'd by many a wound,

. His mangled body 'midſt the ſlain was found.

Myſterious fate! ſcarce was his ſpirit gone

Than ſhouting hoſts proclaim'd the battle won.

Each happy ſoldier too enrich'd with ſpoil,

The ample payment of his martial toil,

Now homeward plods with eager pace his way,

And thro' each village cries, " *We've gain'd the day.*"

Then might you ſee at ev'ry threſhold wait.

The maiden anxious for her lover's fate;

The

The mother her returning fon behold,

And fhrink with horror as his tale he told;

The tender wife, " in tears of tranfport drown'd,"

Her partner meet, and " weep o'er ev'ry wound."

And fo my child; for when the orient ray

Illum'd th' horizon and proclaim'd the day,

On ev'ry path fhe ftretch'd her longing eye,

If haply there fhe might Horatio fpy,

If on the way fome human form appear'd,

Bright hope awhile her throbbing bofom chear'd,

Till nearer feen a ftranger only came,

And double anguifh fhook her tender frame.

At length a ruftic, in whofe fteely breaft

The fofter paffions ne'er were known to reft,

Her

Her ear demanded, and at once declar'd

The dreadful fate her lov'd Horatio fhar'd.

I faw him fall, he cried, and more had fpoke

If more could Anna hear: the fudden ftroke

Her tender frame o'erpow'r'd ; her lips no more

Their former tint of bright vermilion wore;

Clos'd were her eyes, her pulfe with languor beat,

And clammy cold fupprefs'd the vital heat.

Proftrate fhe lay, and ev'ry effort vain,

Till nature, quicken'd with a fharper pain,

Grim death, that lately with uplifted hand

Prepar'd his blow, now check'd by heav'n's command,

A while retir'd, nor durft his victim claim

Till from her womb Horatio's image came.

(In

(In thee, my Henry, now that form I trace,

And in the child I view the father's face.)

But Anna, long by anxious cares oppreſt,

By grief exhauſted, and bereav'd of reſt,

Three nights in pangs of nature's ſorrow lay,

Ere on her infant dawn'd the light of day :

Then frenzy ſeiz'd her brain—" There! there!" ſhe cried,

" I ſee my love with ſtains of purple dy'd.

" Heav'ns, what a fight!—Let vengeance act her part,

" And arm theſe hands to tear the murd'rer's heart.—

" Hark! hark! his well-known voice my ear aſſails—

" He calls—but ah! ſome potent charm prevails—

" Horatio's fled—his wretched Anna left"——

She ſcream'd—and ſunk again of ſenſe bereft.

Life's

Life's quiv'ring light once more it's force refum'd,

And with a tranfient blaze her breaft illum'd;

Reafon her feat regain'd, while, thus expreft,

She gave with fault'ring voice her laft requeft:

    " Thanks be to God, my forrow's nearly done,

" *The faith is finifh'd, and the battle won* *.

" Soon fhall I reach the heav'nly Canaan's fhore,

" My lov'd Horatio meet, and part no more.——

" Father! protect my babe with guardian care,

" His early fteps direct, his heart prepare

" To feek thy face, that, when life's thread fhall ceafe,

" Good Simeon like, he may depart in peace †.

" I afk no more——My Savior, now," fhe cried,

" Receive my foul!"——then fweetly fmil'd, and died.

Such

Such was thy parent's fate ; 'twas God's decree

Maternal care fhould ne'er be fhewn to thee.

Horatio's part I bear, t' inftruct be mine

With love of truth thy heart—to learn be thine.

 Acafto ceas'd—fufceptive Henry ftood

In fix'd amazement, whilft a briny flood

His vifage bath'd, and well his mind exprefs'd,

Tho' paffions ftrong the pow'rs of fpeech fupprefs'd.

But e'er Acafto clos'd the plaintive tale,

A folemn gloom befpread the fertile vale;

Blithe day with all her bufy train was fled,

And Phœbus haften'd to his weftern bed.

Night o'er the land her fable curtain drew,

And dufky tints on all creation threw.

The

The meadows, late in brighteft hue array'd,

Lofe all their gladnefs in the gen'ral fhade;

And, as with fympathetic feelings wrung,

A teary drop on ev'ry bloffom hung.

The pallid lift'ning moon, with quiv'ring light;

But half unveils her waning wat'ry fight;

Salutes with filver'd ray the mournful wood,

And meets her image on the trembling flood;

Hears the fad tale, and, ftruck with forrow deep,

Behind fome friendly cloud retires to weep;

Whilft the fair ftars, attendant on their queen,

The concert join, and twinkle o'er the green.

F I N I S.